Heart Prayers
a practice of personal prayer

KJ Wuest

WIPF & STOCK · Eugene, Oregon

Wipf and Stock Publishers
199 W 8th Ave, Suite 3
Eugene, OR 97401

Heart Prayers
A Practice of Personal Prayer
By Wuest, KJ
Copyright©2011 by Wuest, KJ
ISBN 13: 978-1-93735-803-7
Publication date 4/15/2012

Scripture quotations are from New Revised Standard Version Bible, copyright 1989, Division of Christian Education of the National Council of the Churches of Christ in the United States of America. Used by permission. All rights reserved.

For Paul
"I won't tell you no lie
But there's more to this journey
Than is apparent to the eye."
—STING, "Rock Steady"

Courage is fear that has said its prayers.
--Dorothy Bernard

TABLE OF CONTENTS

Preface	*ix*
Healing and Comfort	2
Hope and Trust	28
Vision and Call	50
Rest and Renewal	80
Resources	*98*
Gratitudes	*100*

Preface

Sometimes life calls for praying by the seat of our pants. During a particularly long hard stretch of cancer treatment for my husband I kept a book of prayers just for him and wrote a prayer or two in it every trip to the clinic—every test, every chemotherapy and radiation treatment, meetings with Doctors—good news, no news, and bad news…little prayers trickled out of me and onto the pages of this small closely held journal. After more than a year of writing prayers for my husband, it occurred to me that it wouldn't be a bad idea to pray for myself in the same way.

    While there are a wide variety of excellent prayer resources available there are not many in the realm of real life praying for ourselves. We learn early to pray for others, and maybe for what we 'want', but not necessarily for where we *are* or for what we *need*.

I started simply. A journal small enough to fit in my bag, or coat pocket, and a pen rubber banded to it. No excuses, just a need and an intention. These prayers were written moment by moment—in the front seat of the car, at the bottom of the stairs before walking out the door to work, in the waiting room at the clinic, in Starbuck's in the company of a of something very large, warm and delicious. I wrote in the moment of need and expressed as directly as I could my prayer for myself at that moment. I found praying for myself was neither as awkward nor as difficult as I thought it might be. It was instead a profound experience and one that help me to see more clearly God's gracious presence, care and guidance.

-KJ Wuest
September 2011—Seattle, WA

Healing & Comfort

*I love you, O LORD,
my strength.
The LORD is my rock, my
fortress, and my deliverer,
my God, my rock in whom I
take refuge,
my shield, and the horn of my
salvation, my stronghold.*
  -Psalm 18:1-2

Companion God,
    you are in each step
    of each day—
But my steps are
    very heavy these days
    and I need your help.
Holy Spirit, Comforter
    Help me to
    breathe in
        HOPE
    and to
    breathe out
        FEAR
    Remind me that
    you are near. Amen.

Holy Spirit, Comforter
Be my everything
NOW!
I can't bear this
pain I've been in.
I can't bear the
idea that this
pain could be my life—
Holy Spirit,
      COMFORT me.
        Amen.

Companion God,
you have
said that I am
yours and you will
be with me step by
    step—
Today my heart is
heavy and I am tired
I see sadness
all around me
as the holiday
lights and music
gain strength.
Help me see you today.
                Amen.

Beloved Friend,
bless this path
before me
I feel my body
drawing up in the
fear of waiting
out this CT scan
and the results
to come.
Beloved Friend,
hold my hand
and walk with me.
           Amen.

Who waits with me if not you?
Hold my anxious heart
and keep my feet
moving on this path—
You are my companion.
                    Amen.

If not for you
I would feel friendless
even as others try
to comfort me.
Only you have my
whole story and
love me in spite and
in the midst and
      because—
Your love is ever and all.
Let me lean into that
incredible love
      and
Let it be enough
AS I WAIT
      Amen.

Redeemer who
marks me with
the sign
of the
cross
forever—
Help me
to carry this
cross and
bear me up even
as I fall.
        Amen.

Listener of my heart—
Hear the roller coaster
of noise
and bring me calm.
Guide my preparations
give me clarity
and economy
of words
that your WORD
would bring comfort
challenge and
promise!
        Amen.

Renewer of Hearts,
you have reached out
and refreshed me
with surprise
today.
Hold my feet to the
ground and set me
on a course of
      healing hope.
Guide me
Hold me
Heal me
      Amen.

Rescue me—
From this pit.
I am at a loss—
Loss of:
    Composure
    Hope
    Spirit
    Strength
I just can't take
any more
open ended
waiting. I want
something that
isn't 'hanging'

Guide me in my steps
that I may
lean on your love.
Hold me.
I am falling.
    Amen.

Give me the words
to meet you today.
Even in my feelings
of discomfort
be my comforter.
Let this darkness pass
bring me your light
to travel by.
>   Be my guide
>   my path
>   my destination
>   my all in all
>   Amen.

Surround me
with your
healing presence
and promise.
Come to me
again and
again
O God.
        Amen.

Remind me Beloved Friend
that you are not
far off.
Draw me
near to
your heart
and
lift my
wavering
spirit and comfort
my sad soul.
For today is only
today—
and you are
everlasting.
        Amen.

Am I alone
standing
between
what surely was
and what
truly could be?
      Where are you, O Lord,
      where are you?
I need your solace—
Your filling of
strong promise
that tomorrow
will come and
you will
hold me into
whatever future
that may be.
      Amen.

Jesus, Prince of Peace,
Do you dream
Peace for me?
You stood and calmed
storms that
raged about you—
What about this
storm that
rages within me?
Help me to see that
you stand with me
and for me
Jesus, Prince of Peace
be my PEACE.
        Amen.

God of Healing,
be not far off!
come near to me
and bathe me with
your LIGHT.
All that is broken
or failing in my
body needs your
tender touch.
Lead me in my LISTENING
that I
    may be more
    more attentive
    and careful of
    my body's needs.
            Amen.

Holy Spirit,
Comforter—
Be with me—
Hold me—
Give me strength

Hold me in the pain
of today
help me to pray
my way
into and
through
all that
is before me.
        Amen.

Pray
Healing
of
body, mind, spirit…
Into your hands,
O Lord,
    I commend
    myself
    to your
    healing touch.
        Amen.

Healing God,
if I could lay
these headaches
in your arms
I would rejoice.
Help me with
the pain
give me guidance
to know my body
and what to
question.
> Help me find a
> new way to
> breathe through
> the pain.
>> Amen.

Wrap me in prayer,
O Comforter
    gather the scattered
    parts of my mind
    and soul
    and wrap me
    in prayer.
Smooth the
    prickly edges
    of today's
    uncertainty
    and wrap me
    in prayer.
You are my comfort.
    Amen.

Tender One
mend me and
lift my heart.
Teach me what would
be healing today.

I am waiting for you—
with you
in you—
Thank you.
        Amen.

Along the path
I listened
for you
but heard
    Silence—
Not from me—
I sought silence
from my noise
    and yearned for
    a word from
    you
but could not
respond,
    "Thanks be to God."
       Amen.

Renewer of Hearts,
take hold of
my heart
and hold it gently
in your restoring
        Love.
I ache with every
fiber of my being—
My chest feels hollow
and in need
of your
tender solace.
        Amen.

Comforter—
>	I ache.

Guide—
>	I am stumbling.

Protector—
>	I feel lost.

Sustainer—
>	I am empty.

Renewer—
>	I need you.
>>	Amen.

Seer and Seeker—
Is the playing field
never level?
Why one more
looming lump
of fear?
We are not over
the last one!
I feel overwhelmed
by the holes
that keep
Appearing—
Will we all fall
one by one?
        Amen.

Hope & Trust

But this I call to mind,
and therefore, I have hope:
   the steadfast love of the
   LORD never ceases,
his mercies never come to an end;
they are new every morning;
great is your faithfulness.
   "The LORD is my portion,"
   says my soul,
"therefore I will hope in him."
Lamentations 3:21-24

God of Strength—
you carry me
when I cannot
even walk beside you.
Help me to trust—
your help—
your presence—
your love—
your path.
        Amen.

God of All—
This cannot be
your plan for me—
I trust that you
have a plan for
    HOPE!
This is a path full
    of hard boulders
    that cause me
    to fall.
Lift me O God.
              Amen.

Tender Friend,
where are you in all this?
I trust you are
beside,
behind,
ahead
and always with me
        BUT IT IS HARD.
            Amen.

God of Love
be not silent
I need your Word—
Speak to me of
LIFE
HOPE
HEALING.
It is hard to
"Count it all joy"
when each day
seems like another
word of
suffering—
Be not silent
but speak to me.
         Amen.

Present One—
There are signs
>of joy
>but they are hard
>to point to without
>seeming nuts:
- People surrounding me in prayer
- Promises in your Word
- The beauty of fall
- Our great kids
- Friends who stand by
- People willing to listen

Let these things make
>and keep me strong.
>>Amen.

Comfort me, O God,
In my anger—
In my weariness—
In my questions—
In my fear—
Comfort and…
…confront me…
with your love
and your will.
        Amen.

Find me in this
darkness—
Hold me in my pain
I need to feel your
presence
your guiding hand.
All is tightly held fear
and even edged anger.
It feels dangerous
to feel angry—
All this I lay in
your arms.
        Amen.

Looking back
is easier
looking ahead
is difficult and holds
fear of the unknown.
All I can do is
look to you.
         Amen.

Here I am Lord—
where are you
sending me?
I cannot see around
the sure
and certain
bend in this road.
I trust you are
with me but
my feet are growing
heavy and
my heart is
in pain.
The leaves are heavy
drifts of red along
the road—scattered
like my tears.
                            Amen.

God of strength—
Hold me in
the wake of bad news
Comfort me in pain
sooth my soul
wipe away my tears
as you have promised—
Be present and helpful!
       Amen.

Guard of my heart—
Let me lean on
you in my fear.
Wrap your arms
of comfort
about me
and assure me
that Love will
carry me through
this day
and the next.

      Amen.

Heart of my heart
on this day of
celebrating love—
help me not to
fear losing the
love of my life.
I know the depths
of love and loven'
I feel for him
comes from your
love for me. I am
only able to open
my heart and life
because you did.
        Amen.

God of waiting
you are my companion
as we wait for
this next test.
Waiting in this unknown
time I wonder
will we really be
burying the
Alleluia on
Fat Tuesday?
      Amen.

I have cried aloud
to the silent watcher
of my life
and my prayer
has been heard.
You come
with
your loving
arms
and uphold
me in your
STRENGTH
despite my
FEAR.
      Amen.

Friend at the edge
of life,
you hold my life
in the palm of your
hand—
Remember me!
do not leave
me without comfort.
Catch me quick
and guide
me in your way of
     HOPE
     TRUST
     LIFE
          Amen.

Silent Friend—
hold my breaking
heart—
Where does this
rocky path lead?
How many more
twist and turns?
Hold me in my fear
        guide my steps
        my thoughts
        my prayers
that I may walk in
        HOPE.
            Amen.

May HOPE
blossom
in me today.
        Amen!

Watcher of my way—
You are ever near…
though I cannot
feel your presence
you are holding me
in your love and strength
I trust you are
watching my path.
                      Amen.

Giver of Life
All eternal
Light from Light
Guide and friend
Companion
Teacher
you are all in ALL
see me through
    the immediate
    the everyday
    the temporary
that seems too much.
            Amen.

Holder of Hearts
lift me gently today—
Life is feeling fragile
and uncertain—
but not without
promise.
May your gift
of Life and Light
outshine
any and all
threatening
darkness
today and always.
      Amen.

Open me to trust you
even as storm clouds
hover—
Lend me your hardy
way of standing
firm
despite doubtful
possibilities.
You are my ROCK
hold me
firmly as this
next door opens.
       Amen.

Vision & Call

*"Do not remember
the former things,
or consider the
things of old.
I am about to do
a new thing;
do you not perceive it?"*
          Isaiah 43:18-19

Courageous One—
you are my strength.
I have been brought
so low.
Pick me up—
Guide me
in your way
your Word
that I may TRUST
for one more
day.
        Amen.

Listener of my heart—
Thank you
for the gift of love
May I reach out
to all I meet
with the promise
of your presence
in all
--even all "this"
       Amen.

Lord of Life—
you know me
through and
    through—
Relieve me of all
that distracts me
from your way
help me to let go
    of all that I
    complain about—
Help me to be
clearly your
hands in all I do.
              Amen.

Strong and Patient One,
befriend me
in my weak and
weary state.
Lift me once again to
my feet
and prepare me in
your wisdom
for the path ahead.
                Amen.

God of the future—
you are my eyes
for all that lay
ahead—
All that is only
    speculation
    from where I stand.
Help me to leave it
to you and to
stand strong here
      for today.
            Amen.

Your Word is a lamp
To my feet—
Burn bright
O Strong Word!
It is rocky and today
I know not
where to turn—
Only can I lean on you
I am nothing without
you and your strong
Word.
Feed me.
Warm me.
Guide me.
Keep me on this path.
      Amen.

You are the Creator!
The mighty Do-er of
NEW THINGS!
Come into my heart
and turn me
afresh to you and
your NEW THING
for me.
      Amen.

Even now, O Guide—
    Help me to trust
    your leading.

Despite this new surprise
shock, disappointing
turn, fear
despite it all
place my feet and
heart on the
path of TRUST.
Trust that your Light
    outweighs
all darkness.
        Amen.

Help me to trust
your guidance, O God—
Help me to trust
your work in me
and in my life.
Sustain and energize me
that I might not
faint under the
ALL.
    Amen.

Heart of my heart—
Hold mine today
and sustain me
in the many
directions I must
    travel
    watch
    pray
    work
    dream
Teach me your way
of love and
      LIFE.
            Amen.

Wise Friend—
Let me lean on
your shoulder
of understanding
as I seek
    direction
    comfort
    strength
for all that I must do
today—and for
all that today holds.
    Amen.

Guide me across this
wilderness—
Show me the way
and sustain me
with your
LIVING WATER
as I am very
thirsty!
      Amen.

Help me to
be still and know
that you are
>	working in me—
>	stirring in me—
>	gifting me—
with all that I need
to walk through
today and
>	into
>	tomorrow—
Whatever they
may bring—
you are there
holding me.
>	Amen.

Surrounding God—
encompass me
with your love
with the
grand sweep of
creation.
Call me back to
myself and
    guide my steps
    refresh my
    body
    soul
    spirit
    for LIFE!
              Amen.

Guide of my Life—
How will I know
when you point
me a new path?
What form will your
hand take this time
I wonder—
- A friend's voice and knowing questions?
- A relentless phrase that stops me from circling by again?

Open my heart to be
      my eyes as you need.
              Amen.

Heart of my heart,
you surround me
with creation—
Beauty—
Experiences—
and like a child
I can choose
what to pay
attention to,
what to let touch me,
guide me and
change me.
>	Help me to
>	discover more
>	today—
>	and you
>	in all
>	the more
>	before me.
>	>	Amen.

Open my heart to
hear your
summoning out
what I shall be—
Or my becoming clues.
is it the water
rushing over the rocks?
is that your voice?
is it the
rustling of
leaves above
my head?
Is that your voice?
Open the ears
of my heart.
        Amen.

Meet me, O God,
walk me toward
your path
for tomorrow.
        Amen.

Friend,
I am in a spiral
sometimes it
feels like a
downward
spiral
and sometimes it
feels like you are
turning it around
and
upward—
all I can say is I want it
to be a spiral
toward and
around you.
Guide my spiral.
      Amen.

Lift my spirit O God!
It is heavy and needs
your solace and care…
You can see what I
can't even dream
that tomorrow
will be different.
Ask me and I will
answer you
guide me and
I will go
lead me for I am
seeking you and
the peace that only
comes from you.
        Amen.

Giver of Light
show me the way
these steps must
be careful and caring.
Lead me with
your wisdom
and light my way
with your
HOPE.
      Amen.

Creator God—
Lift my energy
and prepare me
for the weeks
ahead.
Calm my head and
heart to stay
focused and
aware of what
needs to be done.
Help me
include others
and not over do.
        Amen.

Hand of Life
who holds me
        guides me
        lifts me
        comforts me
Thank you…
for sustaining me
        guiding me
        gifting me
        challenging me
        providing for me.
All that you are
is to be praised!
        Amen.

Guide of my soul,
help me to pay
attention
to your call—
Help me to trust
your way—

Open my heart
to your consolation
and challenge
bless me this day
that I may walk
and serve in
ways that lead to
LIFE.
        Amen.

Bless me with vision
for this new year.
Beginning in the
midst of grief
and uncertainty—
I simply yearn
for your peace.
Meet me today
and in each step—
Hold me
        Lift me
        Guide me.
        Amen.

Lift me, O God
that I might
have vision
for what is
to come—
>	Help me to calm
>	and center
>	and follow
>	your lead—

Open my heart
to your call
and the unfolding
of today.
>	Amen.

Companion,
I need your guidance
I need to know
   the way—
Where will you
lead me?
Show me
give me clarity
and courage
to make the
changes needed.
Open me.
   Amen.

Friend of my heart—
I am taking a leap
opening myself
to a surprising
opportunity
I trust your
guiding hand
in this—
Trusting you will
      meet me
      shape me
      use me
      in my simple
      saying, "Yes"
                  Amen.

Bless to me, O God,
the path before me
and all that
this day holds—
Bless to me, O God,
the path before me—
and all that
this day holds.
        Amen.

Rest & Renewal

*In returning and rest
you shall be saved;
in quietness and in trust
shall be your strength.
            -Isaiah 30:15b*

Give me the strength
to breathe in HOPE
and breathe out
FEAR
To rest in the silence
of your ever present
Love and comfort
give me this strength
for today.
               Amen.

Bringer of Peace,
you are my comfort.
In you I take refuge
hold me in my
letting down—
    Not doing—
    Undoing—
Refresh me with
the kind of
    PEACE
that comes only
from you.
    Drop by drop
    the rain comes
    and in those drops
    are the living waters
    of your peace today—
        Amen.

God of Sabbath—
you are my strength
as I enter these days
of rest.
Help me to lay aside
all that I carry
and simply BE.
        Amen.

Creator God—
you delight in
creativity—
you tickly my being
as I take time to
simply BE and
PLAY.
Refresh me
in these days
     Restore my soul
     Relax my mind
     Remember me
     to myself.
Hold me in my
Not doing.
     Amen.

God, tonight I need rest.
I have gone
to rest and be
renewed.
I loved the mountains
and soaked a bit
in silence—
Now turn me
and bring me
refreshed
and ready
for all that lay
ahead.
Never let me forget
your presence.
                Amen.

Creator—
Create me anew?
No, maybe I'm tired
of being molded.
Set me aside and
let me rest
unfinished
but still
useful?
      Amen.

Can't something
be complete
and whole?
Guide my heart
toward renewal
and peace.
      Amen.

Help me to step softly
between rocks
over streams
and beside
the waterfalls.
        Amen.

Tender Presence—
Your love and mercy
are from
everlasting to
everlasting—
Wrap my very life
in the solace
of that
promise,
O Lord.
     Amen.

Stand beside me
Companion—
Calm my heart
and help me
to hear you
amid all the
voices of this world.
Open my eyes
to the beauty
of this
pine strewn place
and in the
silence that
surrounds me
Speak, O Lord—
Speak.
      Amen.

God
renew me
from the
crown of my head
to the
soles of my feet.
        Amen.

Help me,
O Spirit,
to rest
in your knowing
regardless
of my
uncertainty.
Help me,
O Spirit,
to rest.
Help me
O Spirit!
    Amen.

Thank you God
thank you for
the many
blessings
in my life.

Thank you for
the lifting in
my spirit—
for your hand
of strength
and comfort
that guides me.
                Amen.

Holy Spirit,
Comforter,
breathe on me
and teach me
of rest.
>Guide my breathing,
>rest my muscles
>still my thoughts
>that I might simply
>be held by
>your love
>for this moment.
>>Amen.

Creator God,
bless me in
these desert days—
That I may
rest beneath
blue sky—
be held by the
presence of
the surrounding
mountain—
> Be at peace
> among the cactus
> and mesquite.
>> Amen.

No moment
too small
for you—
Quiet me
and help my
heart to
hear you.
I stood and
asked for one
word of
blessing and
the river responded,
the trees responded,
the blue sky
covered me—
Was that what you
had to say?
        Amen.

Find me in my
slipping down
hold my heart
renew my sight
open my spirit
refresh my trust
be my strength.
               Amen.

Resources

Coffey, Kathy *God in the Moment: Making Every Day a Prayer,* Maryknoll, NY, Orbis Books, 1995

Guenther, Margaret *My Soul in Silence Waits: Meditations on Psalm 62,* Boston, MA, Cowley Publications, 2000

Merrill, Nan C. *Psalms For Praying: An Invitation to Wholeness,* Continuum, 2002

—*Meditations and Mandalas: Simple Songs for the Spiritual Life,* Continuum, 1999

Richardson, Jan L. *In The Sanctuary of Women: a Companion of Reflection and Prayer*, Nashville, TN, Upper Room Books, 2010

Rupp, Joyce *Prayer,* Maryknoll, NY, Orbis Books, 2007

Weems, Ann *Lament Psalms*, Louiseville, KY Westminster John Knox Press, 1995

Wiederkehr, Macrina *Seven Sacred Pauses: Living Mindfully Through the Hours of the Day,* Notre Dame IN, Sorin Books, 2008

Gratitudes

Specials thanks to: my faith community Kent Lutheran Church where it was my joy to serve for ten years. Our journey together in prayer ministry and in life is something I will treasure forever; Pastor Jane E.M. Prestbye, my friend and colleague, whose support, guidance, enthusiasm and vision helped me through more difficult times than she will ever know.

I will always be grateful to Gina Howell for her love, laughter, friendship and much more; to Patty Sharp, Nancy Schmitt, Molly Murphy, Brendan D'Ambrosio, and St. John the Baptist Catholic Church 2007 Faith Life Retreat team; to Kaethe Schwehn for her insight, generous feedback and support.

Every day I give thanks for Kim Williams, Sandy Larsen, Mary Ann Smith, Leslie Johnson & Stu McDonald, Cindy Hughes, Susan Formo, Emily Bumpous and Carolyn Nirk who have all been so generous in sharing their hope, faith, love, laughter and decades of prayer.

To our kids Sarah, Steven, Grace and Mary—who have all taught me so much over the years and whose varied lives of adventure have provided both cause and challenge in my prayer life. I love you all more than you know. Lastly, it is to my best friend and husband, Paul, my greatest debt of thanks is owed for your support and love through everything we have encountered. I'm always loven' you.

www.ingramcontent.com/pod-product-compliance
Lightning Source LLC
Chambersburg PA
CBHW071223160426
43196CB00012B/2391